Elizabeth Keckley's pincushion

Mrs. Lincoln's Dressmaker

The Unlikely Friendship of Elizabeth Keckley & Mary Todd Lincoln

by Lynda Jones

NATIONAL
GEOGRAPHIC

WASHINGTON, D.C.

This book is dedicated to the memory of my ancestors who didn't have the opportunity to tell their stories; and to my mother, Mildred, who encourages me to tell as many stories as I can. —L.J.

National Geographic is grateful to historian Robert D. Johnston, Ph.D., for his review of the text and pictures in layout.

Text copyright © 2009 Lynda Jones

Book design by David M. Seager

NOTE ON THE DESIGN:

The patterns behind the images on the chapter opening pages are from fabrics popular in the mid to late 1800s. Each pattern was chosen to reflect the setting and economic level of the chapter's part of the narrative. For example, the pattern on page 14 is a simple homespun pattern used to introduce Elizabeth's childhood. The fabric patterns become more elaborate as time progresses. Exceptions include the backgrounds on page 52, which is bunting to reflect the election theme, and on page 70, which is taken from the quilt Elizabeth made of scraps of material left over from the dresses she sewed for Mary Todd Lincoln.

The body text of the book is set in Mrs. Eaves. The display text is set in Yolanda Countess.

NOTE ON LANGUAGE:

In Elizabeth Keckley's era, the term "colored" was used to refer to African Americans. The text of *Mrs. Lincoln's Dressmaker* mirrors the language of the times. The name "Keckley" sometimes appeared as "Keckly." For this book, we used the spelling Elizabeth used in her autobiography. The dialogue in the book is quotations taken from sources credited on pages 76 and 77.

Library of Congress Cataloging-in-Publication Data

Jones, Lynda.
Mrs. Lincoln's dressmaker : the unlikely friendship of Elizabeth Keckley and Mary Todd Lincoln / by Lynda D. Jones
p. cm.
Includes bibliographical references and index.
ISBN 978-1-4263-0377-7 (hardcover : alk. paper) — ISBN 978-1-4263-0378-4 (library binding : alk. paper)
1. Keckley, Elizabeth, ca. 1818-1907—Juvenile literature. 2. African American women—Biography—Juvenile literature.
3. Dressmakers—Washington (D.C.)—Biography—Juvenile literature. 4. Women slaves—United States—Biography—Juvenile literature.
5. Lincoln, Mary Todd, 1818-1882—Friends and associates—Juvenile literature. 6. Lincoln, Mary Todd, 1818-1882—Relations with African
Americans—Juvenile literature. 7. Presidents' spouses—United States—Biography—Juvenile literature. 8. Female friendship—United States—
History—19th century—Juvenile literature. 9. Washington (D.C.)—Social life and customs—19th century—Juvenile literature.
10. Washington (D.C.)—Race relations—History—19th century—Juvenile literature. I. Title.
E185.97.K39J66 2009
973.7092—dc22
[B]

2008029314

Printed in U.S.A.

Contents

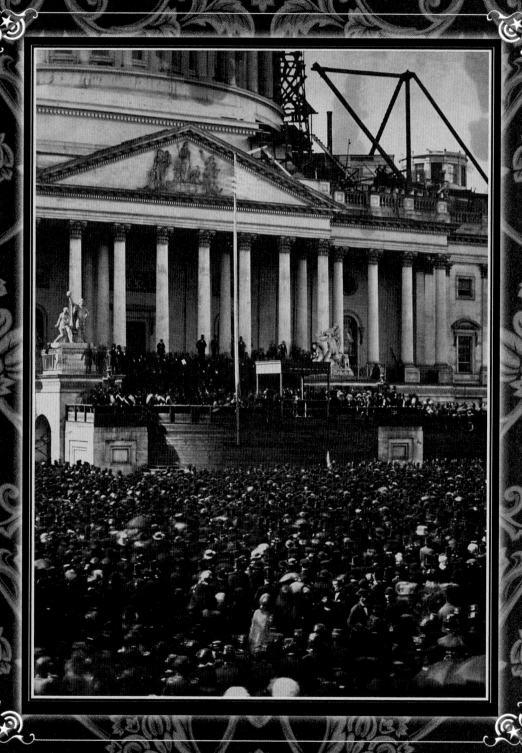

On March 4, 1861, in Washington, D.C., thousands witness Lincoln's
first inauguration ceremony, which took place on the Capitol steps. At the
time, the Capitol dome was still undergoing construction.

CHAPTER ONE

An Invitation to the White House

On the morning of March 4, 1861, Elizabeth Keckley hurriedly left her rooms at the Walker Lewis Boardinghouse and wound her way through the crowded streets of Washington, D.C. It was Inauguration Day. Visitors had traveled from around the nation to see Abraham Lincoln sworn into office as President of the United States. Reporters, politicians, and jobseekers swarmed around Willard's Hotel, where the Lincolns were living until they moved into the White House. Despite the excitement, the city was on edge. Lincoln had received kidnapping and assassination threats, and the nation was about to erupt into civil war. Armed soldiers guarded the inaugural parade route on Pennsylvania Avenue. Sharpshooters took their positions on rooftops. Plainclothes detectives fanned out among the crowds. Cannons were poised, and windows were shuttered.

Elizabeth was not thinking about the inauguration. Her mind was on something more important: her future. The attractive,

*Portrait of Mary Todd Lincoln, whose reign as First Lady
was overshadowed by the Civil War.*

elegantly dressed colored woman, who had been a slave for 37
years, was now one of the most successful dressmakers in the city.
Her clientele included the wives of highly distinguished political and military figures. And today, she hoped to be hired by Mary
Todd Lincoln, the newly elected President's wife. One of Elizabeth's
clients, Mrs. Margaret McClean, had promised to recommend her
services to Mrs. Lincoln in return for a gown she needed made immediately. "I have often heard you say that you would like to work for
the ladies of the White House," said Mrs. McClean. "Well, I have it

Portrait of Elizabeth Hobbs Keckley, who used this picture on her business card to advertise her services as a dressmaker.

in my power to obtain you this privilege." Even though Elizabeth was extremely busy, she made time to make Mrs. McClean's dress. After all, a meeting with the President's wife was her dream.

Mrs. McClean met Elizabeth at Willard's, then instructed her to go to Parlor 6 on the second floor, where Mrs. Lincoln was staying. Nervous, the dressmaker approached the parlor door and knocked. "A cheery voice bade me come in," Elizabeth later wrote, "and a lady, inclined to stoutness, about forty years of age, stood before me."

Mrs. Lincoln was preparing for the Inauguration Day ceremonies.

"You are Elizabeth Keckley, I believe...the dressmaker Mrs. McClean recommended?" asked Mrs. Lincoln.

"Yes, Madam," replied Elizabeth.

"I have not the time to talk to you now, but would like you to call at the White House at eight o'clock tomorrow morning, where I shall then be." Speechless, Elizabeth simply bowed, left the room, and returned to her boardinghouse.

Around midday, the President-elect's carriage rumbled down the Inaugural parade route along Pennsylvania Avenue toward the unfinished U.S. Capitol. Thirty thousand people were gathered on the grounds. The tall, gangly Lincoln, dressed in a black suit, stovepipe hat in hand, stepped out of the carriage, followed by his family. Mrs. Lincoln and the couple's three sons, Robert, Tad, and Willie, sat on the platform on the Capitol steps. The ceremony began, and Lincoln took the oath of office. Then he gave his much anticipated inaugural address.

For Elizabeth, the rest of the day passed slowly. All she could think of was her interview with Mrs. Lincoln the next morning. Her dream to work for the ladies of the White House "was about to be realized, and I couldn't rest," Elizabeth later wrote.

When she arrived at the White House the next day, armed guards were posted outside. The White House doorman checked for Elizabeth's name on the visitors list, and then she was directed to a large waiting room. Her heart sank when she saw three prominent dressmakers also waiting to be interviewed. "With so many rivals," Elizabeth later wrote, "I regarded my chances as extremely small."

Elizabeth was the last person to meet with the First Lady, who smiled and greeted her warmly. "You have come at last!" she exclaimed. Then Mrs. Lincoln asked, "Who have you worked for in the city?"

Elizabeth told Mrs. Lincoln about her clients, including Mrs. Jefferson Davis, whose husband was the President of the Confederate States. Mrs. Lincoln was very impressed and wanted to hire Elizabeth right away. The only matters left to discuss were the dressmaker's schedule and fees.

"Do you have time to do my work?" asked Mrs. Lincoln.

"Yes," Elizabeth began. "Will you have much work for me to do?"

"That, Mrs. Keckley, will depend altogether upon your prices," replied Mrs. Lincoln. "I trust your terms are reasonable. I cannot afford to be extravagant. We are just from the West, and we are poor. If you do not charge too much, I shall be able to give you all my work."

"My terms are reasonable," assured Elizabeth.

Once they agreed on fees, Elizabeth took Mrs. Lincoln's measurements. Then the First Lady handed her a bright rose silk antique gown, which needed to be altered. Mrs. Lincoln planned to wear it to the President's first official White House reception. Elizabeth left for her rooms at the Walker Lewis Boardinghouse and began working on the dress right away.

As Elizabeth was completing the alterations, however, Mrs. Lincoln made some last-minute requests. She wanted the style of the dress changed, and she also asked Elizabeth to sew a blue silk blouse for her cousin. This extra work required more time, and

Elizabeth didn't finish the gown until the evening of the party. When she arrived at the White House, Mrs. Lincoln spat, "You have disappointed me—deceived me. Why do you bring my dress at this late hour?"

Frank Leslie's Illustrated Newspaper, *one of the most popular publications of the time, reported on the array of exquisite ball gowns worn by distinguished ladies at receptions and balls in Washington, D.C.*

"Because I have just finished it, and I thought I should be in time," Elizabeth explained, as the prospect of working with Mrs. Lincoln began to dim.

"But you are not in time, Mrs. Keckley. I have not time to dress, and what is more, I will not dress and go downstairs."

"I am sorry if I disappointed you, Mrs. Lincoln…will you let me dress you? I can have you ready in a few minutes."

But Mrs. Lincoln was adamant. "No, I won't be dressed," she said. "I will stay in my room. Mr. Lincoln can go down with the other ladies."

Mrs. Lincoln's cousin, Elizabeth Grimsley, and her sister, Elizabeth Edwards, gently persuaded her to get ready. When she finally agreed, the dressmaker calmly helped her into the gown, then placed red roses in her hair. Mrs. Lincoln seemed pleased with her appearance, but she did not say a word to Elizabeth.

Suddenly, President Lincoln bounded into the room with two of his sons, Willie, ten, and Tad, eight, and stretched out on the sofa. He was in a playful mood, laughing with the children and reciting poetry, as he pulled on his white gloves and admired his wife. "I declare," exclaimed the President, "you look charming in that dress. Mrs. Keckley has met with great success." Delighted, Mrs. Lincoln smiled, and she and the President headed downstairs. The reception was a triumph, and Mrs. Lincoln received many compliments about her gown. From that day on, Elizabeth was Mrs. Lincoln's official dressmaker, a position that would grow into something far greater than either woman had anticipated—friendship.

When Elizabeth was a young slave, like the one above,
she worked long hours taking care of many household chores, minding the children,
and sewing clothes for her slaveowners' family.

CHAPTER TWO

The Life of a Slave Girl

Sometime in February 1818, on a plantation in Dinwiddie County, Virginia, Mammy Aggy gave birth to her daughter, Elizabeth "Lizzie" Hobbs. Colonel Armistead Burwell, a veteran of the War of 1812, had inherited Aggy and her siblings after his father's death. Mammy Aggy, a slave, was a hard worker, and her many skills made her a valuable piece of property. She took care of the domestic chores in the "big house"—the colonel's home—and cared for the 11 members of the Burwell family. A gifted seamstress, she also made clothes for the entire household, including the Burwells' numerous other slaves. The Burwells fully expected that Lizzie would become as valuable as her mother.

The only father Lizzie would ever know was George Pleasant Hobbs, who was owned by a man on a neighboring farm. Aggy could not bear to tell Lizzie that her real father was the colonel, a secret she would reveal on her deathbed many years later.

Slave marriages were illegal; instead, couples held a wedding ceremony in which they "jumped the broom" in front of family and friends to symbolize their love. Elizabeth's mother, Aggy, and the man she knew to be her father, George, may have practiced this ritual.

But Lizzie, who resembled her light-skinned mother, may have guessed the truth; the fair-skinned girl with her long black hair bore no resemblance to the dark-skinned man she knew as her father. It was common practice for slaveowners to force themselves on female slaves they found attractive. Slaves didn't have any rights, so there weren't any laws to protect them. Though the colonel allowed Aggy and George to marry, the marriage was not legally recognized. These unions were not recognized by the law or the church.

In 1822 financial troubles forced the colonel to sell his farm and find employment. The Burwells moved with their slaves to

Prince Edward County, Virginia, where the colonel took a job as a steward at Hampden-Sydney College. The school, founded in 1776, was attended by the sons of wealthy white families. Slaves were needed to maintain the grounds and classrooms, and prepare and serve meals. The students paid Burwell for the services the slaves provided.

Lizzie's father now lived 100 miles away and was only allowed to visit on Christmas and Easter. One Christmas was filled with tears and sadness. In their crude slave cabin, the Hobbs learned that George and his master would be moving permanently to Tennessee. "The announcement hit like a thunderbolt," Lizzie later wrote. The family was overwhelmed with grief. Though it was against the law for slaves to be educated, Aggy and George had learned how to read and write. The heartbroken couple wrote each other regularly. George's letters usually included a message for his daughter: "Tell my darling little Lizzie to be a good girl, and learn her book [sic]. Kiss her for me and tell her that I will come to see her some day." But George died without ever seeing his family again.

Lizzie was only four when she was given her first task as a slave—taking care of Mrs. Burwell's infant daughter. "My old mistress promised me that if I would watch over the baby well, keep the flies out of its face, and not let it cry, I shall be its little maid," Lizzie wrote. On her first day in the big house, Lizzie began rocking the cradle with great enthusiasm. The child was a "sweet black-eyed baby...my earliest fondest pet," Lizzie recalled. Suddenly, the cradle tipped over too far and the infant tumbled out onto the floor. While shouting for help, the frightened child grabbed a shovel from the fireplace and tried to scoop the baby up and put her back in the cradle. When Mrs. Burwell saw what was happening, she ordered the four-year-old outside to be whipped. The severity of her first beating, said Lizzie, was a painful and lasting memory.

A drop in enrollment at the college led to a decrease in Mr. Burwell's income. As a result, he began selling his slaves to

At this slave auction in Virginia, members of this family could be separated and sold to different buyers. Elizabeth feared that she would be sold and never see her mother again.

make money. He separated wives from husbands, parents from children. With the number of slaves declining, Lizzie's mother had to take on extra chores. To help her mother, the eight-year-old learned how to sew, knit, and handle other domestic duties. Lizzie remembered the work being very demanding: "My young energies were taxed to the utmost." But no matter how hard she worked, nothing she did pleased her mistress. "You'll never be worth your salt," declared Mrs. Burwell.

These words haunted Lizzie. She was terrified when she watched as Mr. Burwell "placed a slave boy on a scale [to] sell him, like the hogs, at so much per pound," she remembered. Would she be next?

Eventually, the mistress had had enough. She separated Lizzie from her mother, and loaned the 14-year-old out to one Burwell family member after another. In 1831, Lizzie was sent to Virginia's Chesterfield County to live with her master's eldest son, Reverend Robert Burwell, and his wife, Anna. Like his father, Robert was struggling financially. Anna was penniless and, as Lizzie soon learned, difficult to please. The couple was too poor to buy slaves of their own. As the sole household slave, "I did the job of three servants," Lizzie complained, "and I was looked upon with distrust."

In 1835, the Burwells moved to Hillsborough, North Carolina, where Anna founded a school for young girls. As 18-year-old Lizzie watched young white girls being educated, she continued her education in what she called the "hardy school" of slavery.

The more she thought about the injustices of slavery, the more sullen she became. Furious with Lizzie's attitude, Anna began a campaign to put the slave in her place with a series of brutal whippings. When Anna's husband refused to discipline Lizzie, she turned to William Bingham, a member of their parish and the village schoolmaster. Lizzie was sometimes hired out as a babysitter for his children.

One day, while at his home, Mr. Bingham ordered Lizzie to come into his study and remove her dress for a whipping. Shocked, Lizzie refused. "Nobody has a right to whip me except my own master, and no one shall do so if I can prevent it." The two struggled, but Mr. Bingham overpowered her. "Oh, God! I can still feel the torture now," she later wrote. Lizzie ran back to the Burwells' home and demanded to know why they had let Mr. Bingham beat her. The reverend refused to explain and told her to go away. But Lizzie wouldn't go. She insisted that the clergyman tell her what she had done to deserve such treatment. The more Lizzie pressed, the angrier he became. Suddenly, he picked up a chair and brought it down across her already raw, bloody back. She was savagely beaten several more times, and with each blow, she bit her lip, refusing to cry out in pain.

Lizzie lay in bed for days while her battered body healed. Filled with shame over the physical abuse, Mr. Burwell promised Lizzie that he would never beat her again. "Though I tried to smother my anger and to forgive those who had been so cruel to me, it was impossible," Lizzie wrote.

Slaveowners regularly whipped their slaves to control or punish them. Elizabeth was brutally whipped for the first time when she was only four years old.

Her torture, however, continued in another way. For four years, Alexander Kirkland, a white merchant who lived nearby, forced himself on her. Her owners did nothing to help her. Around 1840, when Lizzie was in her early 20s, she gave birth to a son whom she named George, after the man she knew as her father.

*This 1846 portrait is the earliest known photo of Mary, who was then
a 28-year-old wife and mother. This photo was taken the same year
Lincoln was elected to Congress.*

CHAPTER THREE

Mary: Kentucky Belle

Mary Ann Todd was part of a large, bustling family. Born on December 13, 1818, to Robert and Eliza Todd in Lexington, Kentucky, she was the fourth of seven children. Her father, a wealthy banker, and his wife were very proud and ambitious people. Their ancestors had named and helped settle Lexington in 1775. Active in the political and social scenes, the Todds were quite prominent.

Mary was a pampered child surrounded by luxury, and had a house full of slaves to cater to her every need. Mary was closest to Mammy Sally, who raised her from birth. It was Mammy Sally who comforted Mary and lavished her with attention.

Mary experienced tremendous loss and sadness at an early age. Her younger brother Robert died when she was three. When Mary was six, she suffered another tragedy. Her mother died while giving birth to her seventh child. Mr. Todd immediately began looking for a new wife to take care of his children. Nearly a year after his

*Mary's bedroom at her home on Main Street, in Lexington,
Kentucky, from the ages of 13 to 21. With such a large
household, Mary had to share her room.*

wife's death, he married Elizabeth "Betsey" Humphreys. The Todd
children despised their new "Ma." Mary regularly disobeyed her
and talked back. She once even put salt in her stepmother's coffee.
"You're a limb of satan loping down the broad road leading to
destruction," warned Betsey.

Betsey and Mr. Todd eventually had nine children together. With
so many young ones underfoot, Mr. Todd barely paid Mary any attention. Mary became increasingly spiteful, moody, and argumenta-
tive. It was with great relief that the Todds sent nine-year-old Mary
to board at Shelby's Female Academy, in Lexington, Kentucky. Five
years later, she continued her education at Lexington's prestigious
Mentelle's for Young Ladies. Mary excelled as a student, and she

loved reading and reciting poetry, speaking French, and learning the latest dances. Mary graduated when she was 19.

Mary was unusually well-educated for her time. Back at home, she discovered that she could use her intellect and interest in politics to attract notice. When she engaged in lively conversations about politics with adults, her father paid attention to her. He valued her opinions. Mr. Todd was a Lexington councilman, and a member of the Whigs, a political party. The family regularly entertained distinguished politicians. Henry Clay, leader of the Whigs and a frequent visitor to the Todds' home, abhorred slavery. Mary supported his views: When Mary discovered Mammy Sally giving food to runaway slaves escaping to freedom in Canada, she kept it a secret. As a result of listening and contributing to the discussions in her home, Mary had developed an understanding of politics that was impressive and unusual for someone her age and gender. Women, however, thought her uncouth. Females were discouraged from expressing their opinions or engaging in serious discussions about any subject with men. It was considered unladylike.

In 1839, eager to escape her stepmother, Mary moved in with her sister Elizabeth and Elizabeth's husband, Ninian Edwards, in Springfield, Illinois. The Edwardses often hosted gatherings for the social and political elite at their mansion. The attractive, fashionably dressed Mary loved being part of the social whirlwind. She attended teas, dinners, and parties, showing off her colorful hoop skirts and satin shoes. The 21-year-old was lively and charming. A gifted conversationalist, she casually peppered her conversation

When Mary was 20, she left Kentucky to live with her sister Elizabeth (left)
and her husband, Ninian Edwards, in Springfield, Illinois. It is here that
Mary married Abraham Lincoln, whom the Edwardses disapproved of.

with French phrases or lines of poetry. She was very popular and as a
result, the southern belle was courted by a bevy of young lawyers and
politicians. But her intelligence, sharp tongue, and keen knowledge
of politics intimidated most men. Besides, these suitors didn't live
up to Mary's expectations, anyway. She was ambitious and craved
being in the spotlight. Mary wanted to be somebody. Her future
husband would have to be able to climb to great heights. "I shall
become Mrs. President," she boldly declared to one suitor upon
dismissing his marriage proposal.

Mary met her match in Abraham Lincoln, a lawyer and state legislator, whom she met through his law partner, John Todd Stuart, Mary's cousin. They were a curious pair. He was tall and lean; she was short and stout. She was from a wealthy, well-regarded family; he was a poor backwoodsman. Mary was an outspoken, naturally social creature who had a high regard for appearances. Lincoln was awkward and shy and didn't care anything about appearances. Still, they had a lot in common. They were highly ambitious and shared a love of politics and poetry. Both were moody, and both knew what it was like to lose a mother at a young age. When the two began courting, Mary's family strongly objected. They dismissed Lincoln as an uneducated country bumpkin. But Mary didn't care what her family thought. She saw Lincoln's potential for greatness, and she was determined to help him realize it. The two had a tumultuous courtship and even separated for a time, but they eventually overcame their obstacles. On November 4, 1842, Lincoln and Mary were married.

Young lawyer and state legislator Abraham Lincoln was attracted to Mary's intellect and wit.

Elizabeth posed for this portrait sometime during the 1860s.
Her wardrobe was as fashionable and elegant as the clothes
she designed for her elite clientele.

Chasing Freedom

Around 1840, Lizzie returned with her son to Dinwiddie County, Virginia, to serve Colonel Burwell's sister, Ann, her lawyer husband, Hugh Garland, and their children. The family lived at Mansfield, a large house that sat along the banks of the Appomattox River. Lizzie was delighted that she and her infant son were only a short distance from the colonel's home, where Lizzie's mother lived. But Lizzie was forced to give up baby George. The colonel wanted the child to be raised by Mammy Aggy.

Lizzie spent four years at Mansfield. During that time, she met James Keckley, a handsome, free colored man who worked in the area. James visited her frequently, and the two fell in love. Eventually, he asked her to marry him. But Lizzie refused. What good could come from their relationship? she wondered. Marrying and bringing another child into slavery was too painful. Any child born to a slave mother was a slave, even if the father was free. As a result, Lizzie decided that she would never get married unless she too was free.

When the colonel died in 1844, Aggy and George joined Lizzie at Mansfield. She was thrilled that her family was reunited. But they were soon uprooted again. Poor financial investments had depleted Hugh Garland's savings, and he moved his family to St. Louis, Missouri. In order to increase his income, Mr. Garland decided to hire out Mammy Aggy as a seamstress. Lizzie was appalled. "My mother, my poor aged mother, go among strangers to toil for a living! No!...I would rather work my fingers to the bone, bend over my sewing 'til the film of blindness gathered in my eyes, nay even beg from street to street," Lizzie later wrote. She convinced Mr. Garland to hire her out instead.

Lizzie, whose mother had taught her how to sew, was a gifted seamstress. Word about her exquisite dresses, gowns, and riding outfits soon spread. She gained an impressive clientele, "the best ladies of St. Louis," and was soon overwhelmed with orders. Though Lizzie regularly moved about the St. Louis area, she needed permission to do so. Missouri law required that slaves have written permission from their slaveowners in order to travel throughout the city or into other states. With this document in hand, Lizzie frequently took the ferry across the Mississippi River to Illinois, a free state, to buy the finest fabrics and trimmings. Her patrons' husbands gave her money to buy whatever she needed. She was a shrewd businesswoman, bargaining with shopkeepers to make the best deals for her clients. And, yet, every penny she earned was turned over to her master. "With my needle, I kept bread in the mouths of 17 persons for two years and five months,"

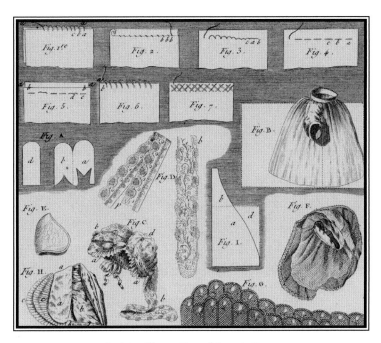

A 1770 illustration of dress patterns.
Elizabeth may have created and used patterns of her
designs for some of her clients.

Lizzie later wrote. She wryly asked herself: Am I, or am I not, now worth my salt?

The punishing workload began to take a toll on her health. More and more, she thought about the evils of slavery. Why should her slaveowners live in comfort while she suffered? she fumed. She wanted freedom for herself, but especially for her son. His skin was as white as their master's, yet he was a slave. "He came into this world through no fault of mine, and yet, God only knows how much I love him," Lizzie wrote. She made up her mind to buy her freedom and that of her family. Her aging mother, however, decided to remain with the Garlands.

In 1847 or 1848, Lizzie bravely walked into Mr. Garland's study and informed him that she wished to buy herself and her son. Then she asked what his price would be. The attorney waved her away and told her not to bring up the subject again, but she persisted. Exasperated, Mr. Garland took a quarter from his pocket and held it out to her. "If you really wish to leave me, take this," he said. "It will pay the passage of yourself and boy on the ferry-boat, and when you are on the other side of the river you will be free."

At this stop on the Underground Railroad,
abolitionist, or antislavery, whites help escaped slaves
continue on their journey northward to freedom in Canada.

"No, master," Lizzie responded. "I do not wish to be free in such a manner. I can cross the river any day, and have frequently done so, but will never leave you in such a manner. By the laws of the land I am your slave—you are my master, and I will only be free by such means as the laws of the country provide."

Mr. Garland was pleased that Lizzie had no plans of leaving illegally. Many slaves had fled to freedom on the Underground Railroad, a vast network of coloreds and whites who helped runaway slaves hide safely until they could continue to the next stop on their journey north into Canada. Others escaped by entering a free state on their own, but they were often caught by slavecatchers and returned to their masters.

Two events may have caused Mr. Garland to grant Lizzie's request to buy her freedom: writing a book on slavery and taking on a historic court case in 1849. He was hired by a woman named Irene, the widow of Dr. John Emerson, and her brother to represent them in a case against the Emersons' former slave, Dred Scott. Born into slavery, Scott sued his owners for his freedom and won. Mr. Garland, however, appealed the case in a higher court and prevailed. The result of his work may have caused Mr. Garland to sympathize with Lizzie. She was elated when he summoned her to his office and said, "You have served my family faithfully. You deserve your freedom. I will take $1,200 for you and your boy."

But how would she raise the money? The Garlands depended on her earnings to take care of the household. As a result, there was not much left to save.

Meanwhile, James Keckley, the man who had asked Lizzie to marry him, had followed her to St. Louis. Again, he proposed to her. This time, Lizzie accepted. With Mr. Garland's promise of freedom for her and her son, Lizzie felt secure about her decision. James and Lizzie were married in 1852. The ceremony took place at the Garlands' house, and Lizzie wore a bridal gown she had made for one of the Garlands' daughters. Still, Lizzie continued to live with her slaveowners, working hard to earn enough money to buy her freedom and that of her son. Her husband lived in another part of the city.

By 1854, Garland was dead, and Lizzie still didn't have the money she needed. Lizzie's friends approached her with a variety

Elizabeth planned to travel to New York City to borrow money from an abolitionist organization that loaned slaves money to buy their freedom.

of ways to come up with the funds. But only one idea stood out: traveling to New York, where an abolitionist organization loaned money to slaves to help them buy their freedom. "At last I had made my resolution to go to New York, state my case, and appeal to the benevolence of the people," Lizzie later wrote. Mrs. Garland, however, thought Lizzie would never return. She demanded that her slave get the signatures of six prominent men in St. Louis who would vouch for her return. If Lizzie escaped, the men would have to pay Mrs. Garland $1,200 for the loss of her property. Though shocked by Mrs. Garland's request, Lizzie easily collected the first five signatures. The last gentleman, however, was just as distrustful as her slaveowner. Even though he agreed to vouch for Lizzie, he believed the abolitionists would convince her to stay in New York. Offended that her word was not good enough for the gentleman, she refused his signature.

Lizzie went home, threw herself on her bed, and cried bitter tears. Her hopes of freedom were completely dashed until later that day, when Mrs. LeBourgeois, a client she sewed for, paid her an unexpected visit. The woman had a solution to Lizzie's problem: She would raise the money and give it to her. But Lizzie would only accept the money as a loan. Mrs. LeBourgeois collected the full amount within weeks. "Like a ray of sunshine, she came, and like a ray of sunshine she went away," Lizzie later wrote. "At last my son and myself were free. Free! Free! What a glorious ring to the word. Free!"

*Mary, Abraham, and their sons, Willie and Tad, return
to their home in Springfield, Illinois, from church.*

CHAPTER FIVE

We Are Elected!

Mary's social status plummeted after her marriage. Lincoln was poor, and now, so was she. For a while the couple lived at the Globe Tavern, in Springfield, Illinois, a crowded, noisy boardinghouse. There was no parlor where Mary could entertain. And when Mary gave birth to her first child, Robert, she had to care for him without the support of slaves. With financial help from Mary's father, the couple eventually bought a house spacious enough for their growing family. Mary's second son, Eddie, arrived in 1846. Life was a never-ending routine of chores: shopping for food, cooking, washing the laundry, and caring for the children. Occasionally, the frugal Lincolns hired servants to help out, but they didn't last long. Mary's demanding ways and short temper would often cause them to flee out the door.

Abe lent a hand with the chores when he could, but he was often away. He spent up to six months out of the year traveling from one Illinois county courthouse to another, trying cases.

Lincoln purchased this home on Eighth and Jackson streets in Springfield, Illinois, for $1,500. In this 1860 photo, Lincoln and his son Tad stand on the porch; Willie perches on the fence.

Mary was lonely, and being alone made her anxious. She was terrified of burglars, barking dogs, and lightning storms, and she suffered from terrible headaches. When Abe was at home, Mary tried to improve his backwoods habits and appearance. She hated when he wiped his dirty hands on his trousers or appeared shabbily dressed. "Why don't you dress up and look like somebody?" she asked.

Though Lincoln enjoyed "lawyering" and being in the state legislature, he longed to be elected to a public office with higher prestige. Mary appointed herself his political advisor. She campaigned on his behalf, rejected positions she thought were beneath

him, offered her opinions, and critiqued Lincoln's speeches.
In 1846 Lincoln won the election for a seat in U.S. Congress. He
lived in a boardinghouse on Capitol Hill in Washington D.C.,
while Congress was in session. Elated by Lincoln's eminent new
post, Mary and the children briefly joined him. She had hoped
to be a part of the Washington social circle, but she was left alone
at the boardinghouse taking care of the children while Lincoln
worked. To entertain herself, Mary shopped, putting everything
on credit. After so many years of penny-pinching, Mary spent
freely. She kept her shopping sprees secret from her husband, but
they were always revealed when Lincoln received the bills.

In February 1850, Mary's life was shattered when four-year-
old Eddie died of tuberculosis. Her father had died the previ-
ous summer, followed shortly by the death of her grandmother.
Grief consumed her. She was inconsolable, and she barely ate.
"Eat Mary," pleaded Lincoln, "for we must live." Mary's behavior
became erratic after Eddie's death. She was more easily frustrated
and angered. She tongue-lashed neighbors, storekeepers, delivery
boys, and Lincoln. In December of that year, however, sadness
turned to joy when Mary gave birth to their third son, William. On
April 4, 1853, they welcomed their fourth and last child, Tad.

When Lincoln's term in Congress ended in 1849, he returned
to practicing law. He remained uninterested in public life until
1854, when he learned of new legislation that would increase the
spread of slavery. That year, Illinois Senator Stephen Douglas

introduced the Kansas-Nebraska Act, which would allow citizens in the new northwestern territories won from the Mexican War to decide if they wanted their states to be free or slave states.

This 1860 campaign poster shows presidential nominee Abraham Lincoln and his running mate, Senator Hannibal Hamlin.

The legislation outraged Lincoln, who believed slavery was a "monstrous injustice" and should not be allowed to spread any further. Lincoln spoke out passionately against the Act. Members of Lincoln's Whig Party, however, were split over the slave issue. As a result, the new Republican Party was formed to fight against the spread of slavery. Lincoln joined the Republicans and made a name for himself speaking on the party's behalf. He became the most prominent Republican in Illinois.

In 1860, Lincoln was nominated to run for President of the United States. Mary's faith in her husband was so great that she began suggesting names of men who could serve in his presidential Cabinet. Southerners, however, were livid. Political leaders from the southern states threatened to secede from the Union if Lincoln was elected. Slavery was part of their culture, they said, and Lincoln aimed to destroy it. If he won, Southerners vowed to break from the Union.

On Election Day, November 6, 1860, Lincoln sat in the Springfield telegraph office waiting for the results. When his victory was certain, the 51-year-old rushed home to tell his wife the good news. As he approached the front door, he shouted, "Mary, Mary, *we* are elected!"

Within ninety days of the President's election, seven southern states had split from the Union, and Mississippi Senator Jefferson Davis had been elected President of the Confederate States. The country was about to engage in the bloodiest war in American history.

Like the slave above, Elizabeth cut fabric and used it to sew stylish gowns, dresses, and riding outfits for her clients in St. Louis, Missouri. As a free woman, she used her skills to create dresses for elite white women in Washington, D.C.

Starting Over

Elizabeth and her 19-year-old son, George, had been living with James Keckley since 1856. It was an unhappy union. Elizabeth learned that her husband, who had claimed to be free, was actually a slave. He was also irresponsible and an alcoholic. After eight years, Elizabeth left him. Then her mother died, and her son left to attend Wilberforce University, a college for colored students in Xenia, Ohio. Elizabeth knew that it was time to leave St. Louis and make a fresh start as a free colored woman.

In 1860, Elizabeth moved to Washington, D.C. She immediately began looking for employment. Armed with letters of recommendations from her former clients, Elizabeth was hired as an assistant dressmaker. Then a new set of challenges threatened her. The law required that a white person confirm to authorities that a former slave was free. She also had to buy a license that would allow her to remain in the city. Without a license, which was $15, she would have to leave the city within ten days. Elizabeth could not afford one, so she explained her predicament to Mrs. Rheingold, whom she sewed for. Her client knew many government officials, including the mayor, who granted Elizabeth permission to stay in the city without a license.

Though Elizabeth only made $2.50 on the days she worked, she was eager to start her own dressmaking business. She rented rooms at the Walker Lewis Boardinghouse, and had business cards and a sign created, which advertised her services. Business was slow at first, recalls Elizabeth, "and I was beginning to feel very much embarrassed, for I didn't know how I was going to meet bills staring me in the face." Elizabeth's fortunes changed when she met the wife of Captain Robert E. Lee during a fitting at Mrs. Rheingold's home. Mrs. Lee needed a gown for a dinner party that would be held at the White House and she hired Elizabeth. Thrilled by the attention her gown had received, Mrs. Lee referred the dressmaker to other ladies. Elizabeth's business flourished. Soon the wives of congressmen, Cabinet members, and senators were clamoring for her services. One of Elizabeth's most loyal clients was Mrs. Varina Davis, the wife of Jefferson Davis, who was soon elected President of the Confederate States. She was so impressed with Elizabeth's skills that she invited her to move south with the family. But Elizabeth politely declined. Having just bought her freedom, her loyalty remained with the antislavery Union.

While Elizabeth sewed, Mary Lincoln set to work making her mark on Washington society. Appearances were very important to her, and as the First Lady, she was eager to act and dress the part. On her first day in the White House, she and the children explored the sprawling 31-room mansion. She was disgusted by what she saw: broken furniture, stained carpets, torn draperies, even rats. Mary decided to transform the mansion into a majestic residence that would symbolize the Union's power. She was delighted that the financing for her project was provided by Congress, which gave each new President $20,000 to make improvements to the distinguished home.

Godey's Lady's Book

Once she became Mary's dressmaker, Elizabeth made sure the First Lady's gowns were highly fashionable, sophisticated, and unique. Mary had extravagant tastes and she loved the French style of dress, which she studied in the popular American fashion magazine *Godey's Lady's Book.* She had Elizabeth make versions of the styles she liked. Elizabeth learned that Mary's tastes were "whimsical" and that she enjoyed suggesting alterations in style. "She always preferred coming to my rooms on Twelfth Street to be fitted," Elizabeth said of Mary, in an interview she later gave to the *Washington Post.* "This becoming known to the public, many a curious crowd awaited her. I often begged her to allow me to come to the White House for fittings, but she would not hear of it."

During Elizabeth's first spring and summer in the White House, she designed and sewed 15 or 16 gowns for the President's

The First Lady wore this white silk gown stitched with flowers and tiny black dots to the Inaugural Ball in 1861.

Mrs. Lincoln in a wide-sleeve, black silk taffeta gown embroidered with leaves and berries in shades of purple, white, green, and red.

wife. Mary's favorite color was white, but she also liked purples, reds, yellows, blues, and pinks. And she preferred plunging necklines and short sleeves. Before every White House affair, Elizabeth helped dress Mary and arranged her jewelry and hair, as well as the bouquet of flowers she carried.

Mrs. Lincoln's activities, opinions, and attire were regularly covered in the press. Reporters made mostly favorable mentions of her gowns. When Mary hosted a White House reception, the *Chicago Tribune* reported: "Mrs. Lincoln wore a very elegant blue silk, richly embroidered, with a long train; also point lace cape, and a full set of pearl ornaments, in which she well sustained the

This skirt and bodice set is made of off-white silk taffeta, with tiny purple flowers stitched between the black vertical stripes.

"Mrs. President" in an off-the-shoulder white gown with ruffles. Tiny rosebuds adorn the ruffles; a garland of roses extends from the gown's bodice.

dignity of her station." The *New York Herald* noted that "Mrs. Lincoln was simply but tastefully attired in white," during a dinner party she gave for Prince Napoleon of France. The reviews of Elizabeth's creations greatly increased the demand for her services. As a result, she had to rent an additional workroom and hire nearly 20 assistants.

While the First Lady and Lizzie were settling into their new roles, the tension between the North and South had reached its breaking point. On April 12, 1861, southern Rebels fired on Union ships approaching Fort Sumter, in South Carolina. The American Civil War had begun.

The war briefly interrupted Mary's plans to refurbish the White House. Confederates had threatened to attack Washington and the Lincoln family. Soldiers secured the White House, camping out inside the mansion and on the lawn. In May, Mary felt safe enough to take one of a series of shopping trips to Philadelphia and New York. Reporters followed her from store to store as she bought the most expensive fabrics, carpets, and furnishings. Merchants told reporters how much Mary had spent. As a result, she was criticized in the press for her extravagance during wartime, when every penny was needed for soldiers' provisions. Mary was humiliated.

Worse, in less than a year, she had exceeded her $20,000 budget by almost half. Unable to convince Lincoln to approve another Congressional grant for her project, Mary took matters into her own hands. She fired staff, swayed merchants into extending her credit, and used her natural powers of persuasion to convince the staff who handled business affairs for the White House to pay her bills.

Mrs. Lincoln purchased this silver tea set for the White House.

For the first time, Elizabeth was not worried about her finances. Her business was thriving, and her gowns continued to earn glowing press coverage. Earlier that year, when Mary was in New York, the *New York Herald* reported that Mrs. Lincoln had attended a ball dressed in "an elegant robe of white grenadine with a long flowing train, the bottom skirt puffed with quilling of white satin, and the apron and shoulders uncovered, save with an elegant point lace shawl. ...Beyond all comparison, she was the most richly and completely dressed lady present." When Mary returned home, she gave Elizabeth yards of fabric and trimming. She then instructed Elizabeth to sew for her a white off-the-shoulder gown, adorned with 60 black bows and hundreds of black dots. Mary planned to wear the gown for a portrait that would be taken by Mathew Brady, a well-known photographer.

In addition to building her clientele, Elizabeth worked on establishing herself in the community. She joined the Fifteenth Street Presbyterian Church, which was attended by many well-to-do colored people. Elizabeth also learned how powerful her association with the Lincolns was. As soon as people found out she was Mrs. Lincoln's dressmaker, Elizabeth wrote, "parties crowded around and affected friendship for me, hoping to induce me to betray the secrets of the domestic circle." But no matter what bribe was offered, Elizabeth insisted that she would never "betray the confidence of [her employer]."

In contrast, Mary had a difficult time making friends in Washington. She was sorely distrusted by the public. Northerners didn't believe that a woman steeped in southern traditions could sympathize with the Union cause, and they accused her of being a Confederate spy. The Southerners called her a traitor. To add to her loneliness, her political partnership with Lincoln seemed to be over. In Springfield, Lincoln had prized her career advice. Now, with his own Cabinet of advisors, he barely listened to her. Mary began confiding in Elizabeth. Mrs. Lincoln criticized her husband's army leaders and Cabinet members, and she revealed her many insecurities: her need to measure up to the social elite in Washington, D.C., her jealousy over any attention Lincoln gave to other women, and her fear that her husband would be killed. "She seemed to read impending danger in every rustling leaf, in every whisper of the wind," Elizabeth wrote. Much like Mary's Mammy Sally, Elizabeth was a comforting presence. With Mary, Elizabeth alternated between hired dressmaker and friend. She calmed Mary when the woman became agitated, consoled her when she was weepy, empathized with her, and offered her opinions. She also took care of Mary's family: She regularly groomed the President's disheveled hair and minded the children.

William Wallace "Willie" Lincoln

When Willie and Tad became ill with typhoid fever, Elizabeth offered to help. Elizabeth and Mary nursed the boys day and night. Tad recovered, but Willie worsened. On February 20, 1862, Willie died.

Elizabeth took time away from her business to console her friend. She understood what it was like to lose a child. Her own son, George, had recently died. He had left college to serve as a soldier in the Union army. But because colored men weren't allowed to fight in the military at the time, her fair-skinned son made the decision to adopt his father's surname, Kirkland, and enlist as a white man. He lost his life fighting in the Battle of Lexington, in Missouri.

"It was a sad blow to me," wrote Elizabeth, "and the kindly womanly letter that Mrs. Lincoln wrote to me when she heard of my bereavement was full of golden words of comfort."

For more than a year, Mary wore black mourning dresses and a heavy black veil. The Union mourned with her. Black crepe draped the White House, and social events were canceled. Mary always feared that the people she loved would eventually abandon her, and that she was being punished by God. She refused to leave her room for nearly a month. She wailed and sobbed. Grief took a severe toll on her mentally and emotionally. Lincoln began to question her sanity. Elizabeth looked on while the President gently led his wife to the window. "Mother, do you see that large white building on the hill yonder?" he asked, pointing to a mental institution. "Try and control your grief, or it will drive you mad, and we may have to send you there."

To help Mary cope with her son's death, Elizabeth introduced her friend to spiritualists, who claimed to be able to contact and communicate with the dead. Meeting with spiritualists had helped Elizabeth with her own loss. Mary was eager. They attended meetings together; sometimes spiritualists came to the White House. Mary later claimed she had spoken with both of her dead sons. Her half-sister Emilie was alarmed when Mary told her that Willie visited her at night, and that sometimes he brought Eddie. Visiting dying and injured soldiers in the army hospitals may have also helped lessen Mary's grief. She brought them treats from the White House kitchen, served food, read to them, and wrote letters to their families. Her kindness lifted the soldiers' spirits and, perhaps, her own.

Lincoln enters Richmond, Virginia, on April 4, 1865, after Union forces win an important victory there. A crowd of jubilant free slaves gather around the President, cheering and hailing him.

CHAPTER SEVEN

Facing New Challenges

In April 1862, Lincoln freed
the nearly 3,000 slaves living in Washington, D.C. That fall,
he issued his preliminary Emancipation Proclamation, a decree
intended to free all the slaves in the Confederate States that had
not returned to the Union by January 1, 1863. But Lincoln had
no jurisdiction over the Confederate States, so the document had
no impact. Still, as Union victories increased, thousands of slaves
fled Rebel states and across Union lines into Washington. Escaped
slaves who became the possessions of the Union forces were called
contraband. The government housed them in makeshift camps
called Freedmen's Villages. Elizabeth, who frequently visited the
camps, was appalled by their conditions. Families lived in tents
or filthy, cramped shanties. Many were ill. They had no jobs,
and they wondered who would provide for them. "They were not
prepared for the new life that opened before them," wrote Lizzie,
"and the great masses of the North learned to look upon your

helplessness with indifference—learned to speak of you as an idle, dependent race." With support from members of her church, Elizabeth founded the First Black Contraband Relief Association, a group of volunteers that assisted former slaves with jobs, clothes, food, housing, and schooling. Elizabeth was voted president of the organization, and branches were eventually formed in Boston and New York. Antislavery organizations in England and Scotland also made donations to assist the slaves.

While traveling with Mary to New York and Boston, Elizabeth mentioned her organization. Mary gladly supported her friend by donating $200. Ministers and colored activists such as abolitionist Frederick Douglass also helped Elizabeth raise funds.

Even though Elizabeth was dedicated to assisting others, she too needed help. Because of the war, the public was practicing "the greatest economy," and her clients were dwindling. Bills were piling up. And she still owed $100 to the St. Louis patrons who had helped her buy her freedom. Ever self-reliant, she offered sewing classes to young colored women and taught them how to start their own dressmaking businesses.

As the elections neared and the war raged on, "much doubt existed in regard to the re-election of Mr. Lincoln," wrote Elizabeth. Mrs. Lincoln was also worried about the future. Elizabeth, who was busy sewing in Mrs. Lincoln's room, noticed that Mary was extremely anxious and agitated.

"What do you think about the election, 'Lisabeth?" she asked.

"I think that Mr. Lincoln will remain in the White House four years longer," Elizabeth replied.

Elizabeth listened as Mary confided that she was worried about money. In order to dress in a way "becoming her exalted position," Elizabeth later wrote, "she had to incur many expenses." Mary purchased expensive fabrics, jewelry, and other goods on credit. As a result, she owed $27,000 to various merchants, and the President was unaware of it. Mary hoped that "good fortune would favor her, and enable her to extricate herself from an embarrassing situation," Elizabeth wrote.

Elizabeth tried to reassure the First Lady of the people's love for the President.

"He has proved faithful to the best interests of the country," Elizabeth said. "The people of the North recognize in him an honest man…He represents a principle, and to maintain this principle the loyal people of the loyal States will vote for him."

"Your confidence gives me hope," Mary replied.

Elizabeth was so sure of the President's re-election that she asked Mary for a favor. She requested the right-hand glove the President would wear at the first public reception, where he would shake thousands of hands. When Mary asked why, Elizabeth replied: "I shall cherish it as a precious memento of the second inauguration of the man who has done so much for my race."

Not willing to leave Lincoln's re-election to chance, Mary returned to campaigning on her husband's behalf. "The White House was besieged with all grades of politicians," wrote

Elizabeth. Mary planned to use her position as First Lady to influence political acquaintances to vote for her husband. In return, she promised these men access to the President, favors, and jobs. She hoped her actions would deliver large blocks of votes for the Republican Party. When Elizabeth asked Mary if the President was aware of her plan, Mary responded, "God! no; he would never sanction such a proceeding, so I keep him in the dark. He is too honest to take the proper care of his own interests."

Mr. Lincoln was admired for "the nobility of his soul and the greatness of his heart," wrote Elizabeth. "His wife was different."

Meanwhile, Union victories in Georgia and Virginia signaled that the end of the war was near. On November 8, 1864, Election Day, "all of my predictions were verified," wrote Lizzie. "The loyal States decided that Mr. Lincoln should continue at the nation's helm." One of Lincoln's first duties after being reelected was to urge Congress to pass a constitutional amendment banning slavery throughout America. On January 31, 1865, the 13th Amendment was passed. If the Union were victorious in the war, the amendment would become law for the entire country and mark the end of two hundred and fifty years of slavery.

That spring, thousands turned out to witness the second Inauguration. Elizabeth arrived at the White House to dress Mrs. Lincoln for the first grand reception of the season. When the President walked into Mary's room, Elizabeth congratulated him. "Well, Madam Elizabeth, I don't know whether I should be thankful or not," he said. "The position brings with it many trials."

The re-elected President takes the oath of office for a second time on March 4, 1865.

As the Lincolns prepared for the reception, large crowds of people filled the rooms and halls of the White House, eager to shake the President's hand. "Many colored people were in Washington, and large numbers had desired to attend the levee..." wrote Elizabeth. But the staff issued orders not to admit them. An exception was made for the eloquent civil rights leader Frederick Douglass, who was invited inside by a member of Congress to greet the President. "Mr. Douglass was proud of the manner in which Mr. Lincoln received him," wrote Elizabeth. "On leaving the White House, he came to a friend's house where a reception was being held, and he related the incident with great pleasure to myself and others."

Two days after the reception, the Lincolns hosted their second Inaugural Ball. Elizabeth created an exquisite dress for her friend:

a white satin gown with an overlay of white point lace, and puffs of silk. She carried a fan of ermine with silver spangles, and wore white gloves, a pearl necklace, and pearl earrings. Her swept-back hair was adorned with white jasmine and purple violets. Neither the President nor Mrs. Lincoln knew it was the last formal affair they would attend together.

In early April, the Union won an important victory: The soldiers captured Richmond, the capital of Virginia. Elizabeth was in her reception room with a client when she learned the good news. She rejoiced and ran to her workroom to share the news with her assistants. But the girls had already heard what had happened. "They were particularly elated, as it was reported that the rebel capital had surrendered to the colored troops," Elizabeth wrote. Elizabeth had promised them a holiday if Richmond surrendered. "I joined my girls in the joy of a long-promised holiday," she wrote. "We wandered about the streets of the city with happy faces."

Elizabeth was touched and delighted when Mary invited her to accompany the Lincolns to Virginia, where the President would survey Richmond and other areas in the state. Perhaps Mary knew how symbolic it would be for Elizabeth to return to Virginia as a free woman. "A birthplace is always dear," Elizabeth wrote, "no matter what circumstances you were born under."

Once in Richmond, Elizabeth and the President's party entered the capitol building. Elizabeth observed broken desks and scattered papers, one of which was a resolution prohibiting free

On March 23, 1865, thousands celebrate the end of the
four-year war by watching the Civil War Victory Parade
along Pennsylvania Avenue.

colored people from entering Virginia. In the senate chamber, wrote Elizabeth, "I sat in the chair that Jefferson Davis sometimes occupied." When the party arrived in Petersburg, Elizabeth wandered off. "I found a number of old friends," she said, but painful memories about her life as a slave returned. "I was not sorry to turn my back again upon the city."

On April 9, the Confederate army surrendered. After four long years, the Civil War was finally over. Northerners cheered. Bands played, fireworks flared, and bonfires crackled.

*Actor John Wilkes Booth fires at President Lincoln
in his theater box during a play at Ford's Theater, in
Washington, D.C.*

CHAPTER EIGHT

Fighting to Survive

Elizabeth saw Mary briefly on the morning of April 14. "She told me that she was to attend the theater that night with the President," wrote Elizabeth, "but I was not summoned to assist her with her toilette." At 11 p.m. that night, Elizabeth was awakened by a friend who had startling news: The President had been shot. "When I heard the words I felt as if the blood had been frozen in my veins," wrote Elizabeth. She went out into the streets, which were alive with rumors and "wondering, awe-stricken people." Elizabeth woke her landlord and his wife, the Lewises, who were good friends. She explained what had happened. "I told them that I must go to the White House," wrote Elizabeth. The Lewises tried unsuccessfully to keep her calm. They dressed quickly and walked with Elizabeth to the White House, which was heavily guarded by soldiers. When Elizabeth saw a kindly old gentleman, she asked him if the President was dead. He replied: "Not dead, but dying." Elizabeth learned that

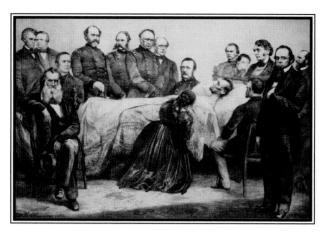

Lincoln lies on his deathbed, surrounded by government officials, family, and friends.

the President had been shot in the Lincolns' theater box and was not expected to live. "We returned home with heavy hearts," wrote Elizabeth. "I could not sleep. I wanted to go to Mrs. Lincoln, as I pictured her wild with grief. Never did the hours drag so slowly."

The next morning, a carriage arrived to take Elizabeth to the White House. The President was dead. Elizabeth entered the darkened room where Mary lay in bed, tossing and turning, "exhausted with grief."

"Why did you not come to me last night?" asked Mary. "I sent for you."

"I did try to come to you, but I could not find you," Elizabeth replied.

She later learned that Mary had immediately sent White House messengers for her, but for some reason they were unable to find her residence.

Tears streamed down Elizabeth's face when she entered the room where the President's body lay. "No common mortal had died," she later wrote. "The Moses of my people had fallen."

While the country mourned Lincoln, Mary remained secluded in her room, weeping. Except for her children, "she denied admittance to almost everyone, and I was her only companion… in the days of her sorrow," said Elizabeth. She stayed with Mary for five weeks, while the newly sworn-in President Andrew Johnson waited impatiently for Mary's departure. Meanwhile federal troops had cornered Lincoln's assassin, John Wilkes Booth, in a Virginia barn. There they shot and killed him.

Unlike Elizabeth, Mary was not fond of keepsakes. Any physical reminders of her loved ones upset her. She gave away Lincoln's belongings, just as she had done with Willie's. "The articles were given to those who were regarded as the warmest of Lincoln's admirers," wrote Elizabeth. To Elizabeth, Mary gave her blood-spattered cloak and matching bonnet worn the night of his assassination, Lincoln's overshoes, and his gold watch. Mary also gave her the President's comb and brush, which Elizabeth had so often used to groom the man's hair.

Mary refused to return to the Lincolns' home in Springfield, Illinois; there were too many reminders of her dead husband and sons. Instead, she decided to start afresh in Chicago. Robert and Elizabeth packed Mary's 64 trunks and hundreds of boxes. Mary implored Elizabeth to come and stay with her until she was settled, but Elizabeth refused.

Lincoln's gold watch

"You forget my business, Mrs. Lincoln," she said. "I cannot leave it." Elizabeth had a huge order for a bridal trousseau to fill the following week. Mary persisted. "You may find it in your interest to go," Mary said. "I am very poor now, but if Congress makes an appropriation for my benefit, you shall be rewarded." Elizabeth insisted that she was not interested in the reward, but she gave in to her friend's demands. "I had been with her so long, that she had acquired great power over me."

In May, Elizabeth, Mary, and her two sons, Robert and Tad, traveled by railcar to Chicago. Finding the city too expensive, Mary rented rooms outside of town. Elizabeth spent a lot of time in Mary's room, "talking with her, contrasting the present with the past, and drawing plans for the future," wrote Elizabeth. During that time, Mary refused to communicate with any other friends or her relatives, "saying that she wished to lead a secluded life for the summer."

By mid-June, Elizabeth had returned to Washington. Mary wrote her nearly every day, complaining about her impoverished state. Mary believed that her debts now totaled $70,000. Because Lincoln left no will, she would receive $1,700 annually from his estate until his financial affairs were settled. Though Elizabeth worried about her friend, she concentrated on reestablishing her business. She was concerned about her own finances. The government had paid for Elizabeth's travel and lodging expenses, as well as $35 a week for taking care of Mrs. Lincoln during her bereavement. But the sum, $360, was far less than Elizabeth could have earned sewing for her clients.

It was with great surprise that Elizabeth saw her slave past catch up with her. She received a letter from her former slaveowner's family, the Garlands: The children and Mrs. Garland wanted to see her. They invited her to Rude's Hill, Virginia, for a visit. Lizzie was delighted. Her friends, however, could not understand why she would visit those who had enslaved her. Elizabeth responded: "To the past belongs that golden period, the days of childhood." Elizabeth's childhood had been anything but golden. Still, she went, perhaps to show the Garlands how successful she had become in spite of their cruelty. When she arrived, she "was shown every attention," she wrote. Her association with the Lincolns and her prosperous dressmaking business had made her a minor celebrity. Elizabeth had finally proved to her former slaveowners that she was worth her salt.

In the spring of 1867, Elizabeth received an urgent letter from Mary. Her financial situation was so dire, she wrote, that she had decided to sell her old gowns, furs, and jewelry to earn money on which to live. For this scheme, she needed Elizabeth's help. "I consented to render Mrs. Lincoln all the assistance in my power," wrote Elizabeth, because she was "the wife of President Lincoln, the man who had done so much for my race, and I could refuse to do nothing for her." Mary asked that Elizabeth meet her in September in New York and secure rooms at the St. Denis Hotel under an assumed name, Mrs. Clarke. Mrs. Lincoln wanted to conduct her affairs incognito. This worried Elizabeth. "I knew it would be impossible for me to engage rooms at a strange hotel for a person whom the proprietors knew nothing about," Elizabeth wrote. She did not feel comfortable with Mary's strange plan, she said, and she hoped Mary would change her mind. But Mary was adamant. "Come by next train without fail. Come, come, come," she wrote, when learning that Elizabeth had not yet left Washington.

Mary arrived in New York before Elizabeth. The two middle-aged women were given the worst rooms on the top floor. "I never expected to see the widow of the President in such humble, dingy quarters," wrote Elizabeth.

The next morning, Mary and Elizabeth sat on a bench in Union Square Park. There, Mary explained how her plans to sell her goods under an assumed name had failed: When Mary arrived in New York she selected a diamond brokerage firm to appraise her goods. Donned in her black widow's dress and veil, she paid a visit to the merchants William Brady and Samuel Keyes. As soon as she handed over a diamond ring inscribed with her name, Mary's true identity was revealed.

The brokers, however, were delighted to have Mary as a client. Her celebrity, they assured her, would increase the value of her property. The brokers were confident that they could raise $100,000 for her goods in just a few weeks. "Mrs. Lincoln was very anxious to dispose of her things, and return to Chicago as quickly and quietly as possible," Elizabeth wrote, "I regret to say, she was guided by their counsel."

The duo pressed Mary into writing letters about her clothing sale to politicians whom Lincoln had done favors for. If the

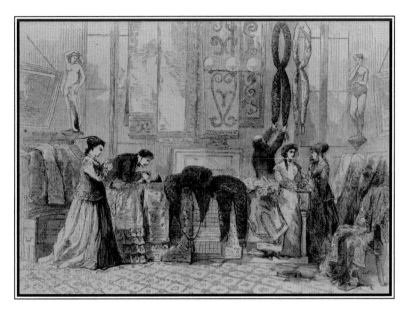

An illustration of Mary Lincoln's wardrobe sale in New York appeared in this 1867 issue of Harper's Weekly.

politicians refused to help Mary financially, the brokers would threaten to release the letters to the press. They believed the men would be embarrassed if the public found out that they had refused to assist Lincoln's widow, forcing her to sell her garments. As Mary wrote, Elizabeth stood by her side, suggesting "that they be couched in the mildest language possible." But Mary did as she wished. The politicians refused to help, and her letters were promptly published in the press. Now that Lincoln was dead, she no longer had any influence over anyone.

Mary and Elizabeth also tried selling the garments to second-hand clothes dealers. Like undercover spies, they traveled around town with the clothes in a darkened horse carriage to avoid being recognized. "There was much curiosity at the hotel in relation to us, as our movements were watched, and we were regarded with suspicion," wrote Elizabeth.

But no matter whom Mary and Elizabeth approached, the merchants had little interest in Mary's wares. Desperate, she accepted whatever they offered. "We returned to the hotel more disgusted than ever," wrote Elizabeth. Lagging sales led Mary to agree to an even bolder move: a public auction of her goods.

Humiliated, she returned to Chicago. Elizabeth remained in New York to supervise the sale, organized by the diamond brokers. Mary wrote frequently. "My dear Lizzie, do visit Mr. Brady each morning at 9 o'clock and nudge them all you can...How much I miss you, tongue cannot tell...I consider you my best living friend, and I am struggling to be enabled some day to repay you." Mary had often told Elizabeth that she would like to take care of her for the rest of her days. She hoped Congress would grant her the remainder of Lincoln's four-year salary. If successful, she would receive $25,000 for each of the four years of his second term minus the six weeks he had served. "If Congress provides for me," she repeatedly promised, "I will provide for you." She also planned to share the commission from the clothes sale with Elizabeth.

But the auction failed miserably. Hundreds of curious onlookers inspected the shawls, dresses, and furs put on display at 609 Broadway. Reporters noted that Mary's clothes were sweat-stained, frayed, and soiled. Many women thought her dresses were too low-cut to wear. Worse, the press published harsh articles criticizing "Mrs. Lincoln's Second-hand Clothing Sale." Mary was called a national disgrace, greedy, and vulgar. Some said she was insane and had been so for years.

So much criticism and misinformation had been written about Mary that Elizabeth took matters into her own hands. She sent a letter to the New York *Evening News,* defending her friend's right to sell her wardrobe. The letter was published on October 12, 1867. Next, Elizabeth asked prominent colored leaders to consider raising funds for her friend. She even planned to sell the Lincoln mementos that Mary had given her. But none of these schemes were successful. Elizabeth, who had shut down her business for three months to help her friend, packed up Mary's unsold goods and sent them back to Chicago.

Elizabeth's finances were now also in dire straits. In order to make a living, Elizabeth wrote, "I was compelled to take in sewing to pay for my daily bread. My New York expedition has made me richer in experience, but poorer in purse. During the entire winter, I have worked early and late, and practised [sic] the closest economy. Mrs. Lincoln's business demanded much of my time, and it was a constant source of trouble to me."

By this time, Elizabeth had read in the newspaper that Mary had been awarded her inheritance from Lincoln's estate: $36,000. Elizabeth probably hoped that Mary would share her good fortune, as she had promised so often in her letters. But the dressmaker didn't receive anything.

This photo of Elizabeth Keckley was taken in the
1890s while she was serving as a domestic sciences teacher at
Wilberforce University, in Xenia, Ohio.

Elizabeth Takes a Stand

lizabeth struggled with how her role in the Old Clothes Scandal, as it was called, would be perceived. Her character and reputation, which she had worked so long and hard to build, was at stake. Elizabeth thought about the striking events in her life that had led to her position as the First Lady's dressmaker. "I have often been asked to write about my life," Elizabeth wrote, "as those who know me know that it has been an eventful one." Profits from a book, she reasoned, could help Mary pay down her debts. More important, the book would explain Elizabeth's role in the scandal.

It's unclear how she attracted the interests of the publisher G. W. Carleton & Company. The publishers hired Jonathan Redpath, a well-known antislavery writer and editor, to help the dressmaker craft her manuscript. Elizabeth wrote down her recollections, and they worked together in Elizabeth's rooms during the afternoons or evenings. To prove her relationship with Mary was authentic, she loaned him 23 letters Mary had written to her. Redpath assured Elizabeth that he would not include anything that would embarrass the Lincolns. The book, published in the spring of 1868, received a great deal of publicity. But when people began reading it, there was an uproar.

Whether intentional or not, Mary's letters appeared in the book. Many of the dressmakers' friends—colored and white—were outraged. Coloreds worried that white employers would no longer hire or trust them. Whites dismissed the book as "backstairs gossip," and declared that Elizabeth was too uneducated to have written it. Mary's son Robert was enraged that she had revealed private information about his parents' relationship. He demanded that the publisher recall the books, and he instructed his friends to buy and burn every last copy. Elizabeth never earned a profit from the book, and the letters she gave to Redpath were never returned to her. Even worse, a vicious racist parody of her book was soon published, entitled *Behind the Seams: by a nigger woman who took in work for Mrs. Lincoln and Mrs. Davis.* Stunned, Elizabeth wrote a letter in her defense and sent it to her publisher, who forwarded it to the *New York Citizen* newspaper. In the letter, Elizabeth wrote: "As I was born to servitude, it was no fault of mine that I was a slave; and, as I honestly purchased my freedom, may I not be permitted to express, now and then, an opinion becoming a free woman?"

No matter how Elizabeth tried to explain herself, however, her reputation had been ruined. Mary and "the colored historian," as Mary would later refer to her, never saw each other again. Mary

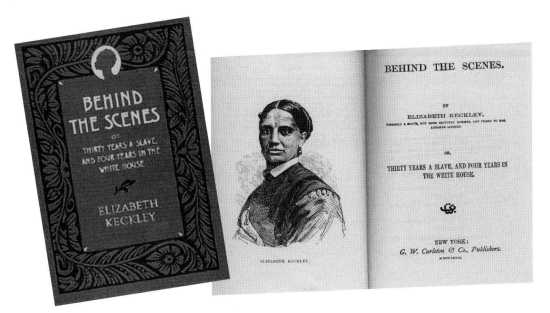

Elizabeth published her autobiography, Behind the Scenes, *in 1868. The book chronicled her life as a slave, her years as Mary's friend and dressmaker, and the Old Clothes scandal.*

believed the one person she had trusted had deceived her.

Overwhelmed by the latest scandal in her life, Mary and her son Tad left the United States in early October 1868, to travel abroad in Europe. When she returned in 1871, Tad became gravely ill and died. This seemed to be the final blow to Mary's sanity. Her behavior became more peculiar than ever. She claimed that she heard voices, that there were steel wires in her head, and that her son Robert was trying to kill her. She sewed $56,000 worth of government bonds inside her petticoats. Convinced that his mother was insane, Robert had her committed to a mental institution. Mary attempted suicide and never forgave her son.

Four months later, she had engineered her release with the help of a lawyer. She returned to Europe until her health began to steadily decline. In 1880 she returned to Springfield, Illinois, to live with her sister, Elizabeth. Mary secluded herself in her darkened bedroom. She died on July 16, 1882, and was buried in a vault next to her husband and sons in Springfield, Illinois.

It is unclear when Elizabeth returned to Washington, D.C., from New York. But once back in the city, she resumed her dressmaking business and taught sewing. Sadly, her business never regained the level of success that she had worked so long and hard to achieve. In 1892, she relocated to Xenia, Ohio, where she taught sewing and domestic sciences at Wilberforce University, the college her son, George, had attended. Always fond of mementoes, she would often give students scraps of fabric that she had saved from the dresses she had sewed for Mary. Elizabeth made a quilt from pieces of the fabrics.

Six years later, Elizabeth returned to Washington, where her stellar success as a dressmaker and businesswoman had begun, and where she and Mary Lincoln had been friends. Perhaps being surrounded by memories of happier times gave the 80-year-old some comfort. She kept busy, teaching and sewing for as long as her eyes and hands remained strong. When she retired, the seamstress moved into a small, sparsely furnished room with only one window, in the basement of the Home for Destitute Women and Children. Elizabeth spent her remaining days gazing out of the window, taking carriage rides, and reminiscing about better days. Above Elizabeth's dresser was a photograph of her friend Mary Lincoln. Elizabeth Hobbs Keckley died at the age of 89 on May

Elizabeth made this quilt with leftover scraps of material that
she used to stitch Mary's dresses. It is 85 1/2 inches square.

26, 1907. In 1960, developers dug up the graves in Old Harmony
Cemetery, in Washington, where Elizabeth was buried. Her
unclaimed remains were moved to another cemetery and placed
in an unmarked grave. Elizabeth's final resting place is unknown.

Still, Elizabeth's contributions to fashion and history live on.
Her life is documented in biographies about notable African
American women, in books recording her life story, and through
Elizabeth's own words in her compelling autobiography.

Author's Note

Elizabeth Hobbs Keckley is a striking historical figure. While I knew of her contributions to fashion, it wasn't until I read a brief biography about Elizabeth's remarkable life that I was moved to learn more about her and, ultimately, tell her story. Elizabeth was proud, fearless and resourceful, and her determination to succeed was inspiring. Most important, she refused to believe what others said about her: that she was inferior and would never amount to much. Still, it's extraordinary that Elizabeth was able to give voice to her own thoughts and feelings about her life by writing and publishing her autobiography: *Behind the Scenes, or, Thirty Years a Slave, and Four Years in the White House.* Most slaves were illiterate; it was against the law for them to learn how to read or write. Without Elizabeth's words to guide me, recreating her life story would have been impossible. My subject's autobiography is the main source of information about her, and nearly all of the dialogue is from her book. Self-taught, self-made, and utterly self-reliant, Elizabeth represents an important but forgotten slice of history that I'm thrilled to be able to share with readers.

Bibliography

BOOKS

Baker, Jean H. *Mary Todd Lincoln: A Biography.* New York: Norton, 1987.

Brown, Hallie Q. *Homespun Heroines and Other Women of Distinction.* New York: Oxford University Press, 1988.

Fleischner, Jennifer. *Mrs. Lincoln and Mrs. Keckly: The Remarkable Story of the Friendship Between a First Lady and Former Slave.* Broadway Books, 2003.

_____. *Mastering Slavery: Memory, Family, and Identity in Women's Slave Narratives.* New York: New York University Press, 1996.

Freedman, Russell. *Lincoln: A Photobiography.* Clarion Books, 1987.

Gernon, Blaine Brooks. *The Lincolns in Chicago.* Chicago: Ancarthe Publishers, 1934.

Hull, Mary. *Mary Todd Lincoln: Tragic First Lady of the Civil War.* Enslow Publishers, 2000.

Keckley, Elizabeth Hobbs. *Behind the Scenes, or, Thirty Years a Slave, and Four Years in the White House.* New York: G.W. Carleton & Co, 1868. Reprinted edition by Penguin Books, 2005.

Kickley, Betsey (pseud.). *Behind the Seams, by a nigger woman who took in work from Mrs. Lincoln and Mrs. Davis.* New York, National News Co., 1868.

Kunhardt, Philip B. *Lincoln: An Illustrated Biography.* New York: Knopf: Distributed by Random House, 1992.

Lowenberg, Bert James and Ruth Bogin. *Black Women in Nineteenth-Century American Life: Their Words, Their Thoughts, Their Feelings.* Pennsylvania University Press, 1976.

Randall, Ruth Painter. *Mary Lincoln: Biography of a Marriage*. Little, Brown, 1953.

Ross, Ishbel. *The President's Wife: Mary Todd Lincoln; A Biography*. Putnam, 1973.

Rutberg, Becky. *Mary Lincoln's Dressmaker: Elizabeth Keckley's Remarkable Rise from Slave to White House Confidante*. New York: Walker, 1995.

Sandburg, Carl. *Mary Lincoln, Wife and Widow*. Harcourt, Brace, Co., 1932.

Simmons, Dawn Langley. *A Rose For Mrs. Lincoln: A Biography of Mary Todd Lincoln*, Beacon Press, 1970.

Smith, Sidonie and Julia Watson, editors: *De/colonizing the Subject: The Politics of Gender in Women's Autobiography*. University of Minnesota Press, 1992.

Turner, Justin G. and Linda Lovitt Turner. *Mary Todd Lincoln, Her Life and Letters*. New York: Knopf, 1972.

Washington, Dr. John E. *They Knew Lincoln*. New York: Dutton, 1942.

Williamson, Joel. *New People: Miscegenation and Mulattoes in the United States*. Free Press, 1980.

DVDs

American Experience—Abraham and Mary Lincoln: A House Divided. PBS, DVD, 2005

NEWSPAPERS

New-York Citizen, October 5, October 9, 1867

New York Herald, October 4, October 14, 1867

Washington Post, October 14, 1900

Sources for Quotes

All quotes were taken from *Behind the Scenes, or, Thirty Years a Slave, and Four Years in the White House*, by Elizabeth Keckley except for the following:

Page 24: "You're a limb of satan loping down the broad road leading to destruction." Baker, Jean. *Mary Todd Lincoln: A Biography*. Page 30.

Page 38: "Why don't you dress up and look like somebody." Baker, page 133.

Page 39: "Eat Mary, for we must live." Baker, page 126.

Page 41: "Mary, Mary, we are elected!" Baker, page 162.

Page 46: "Mrs. Lincoln wore a very elegant blue silk, richly embroidered,..." *Chicago Tribune*, May 10, 1861.

Page 47: "Mrs. Lincoln was simply but tastefully attired in white." Rutberg, Becky. *Mary Lincoln's Dressmaker: Elizabeth Keckley's Remarkable Rise from Slave to White House Confidante*. Page 56.

Pages 48–49: "an elegant robe of white grenadine with a long flowing train, ..." Rutberg, page 61.

Page 72: "As I was born to servitude,..." Fleischner, Jennifer. *Mrs. Lincoln and Mrs. Keckly*. Page 317.

Page 72: "the colored historian" Turner, Justin G. and Linda Lovitt Turner. *Mary Todd Lincoln, Her Life and Letters*. Page 476.

Index

Illustrations Credits

THROUGHOUT: Fabric backgrounds and needle and thread icon: Shutterstock.
FRONT COVER: (Mrs.Keckley) Prints and Photographs Department, Moorland-Spingarn Research Center, Howard University; (picture frames), BigStockPhoto.com; (Mrs. Lincoln), Bettmann/Corbis; (thimble), Radius/Photolibrary; (measuring tape), Scott Rothstein/Shutterstock; (dress form), dafne /Shutterstock; (scissors), john330 /Shutterstock

LOC= Library of Congress; LFF= Lincoln Financial Foundation; Granger= The Granger Collection, NY

3, Cook Family Papers, Manuscript Department, Moorland-Spingarn Research Center, Howard University; 5, David Merewether/ Dorling Kindersley/ Getty; 6, LOC; 8, LFF; 9, LFF; 12, LOC; 14, Private Collection, Peter Newark American Pictures/ The Bridgeman Art Library International; 16, North Wind Picture Archives/ Alamy; 18, Granger; 21, Granger; 22, LOC; 24, M.S. Rezny Photography courtesy Mary Todd Lincoln House, Lexington, KY; 26 left, The Granger Collection, New York; 26 right, George Eastman House/Getty Images; 27, Corbis; 28, Prints and Photographs Department, Moorland-Spingarn Research Center, Howard University; 31, Corbis 32, Granger; 34, Corbis; 36, From the book, "Abraham Lincoln The Boy-The Man", Author Lloyd Ostendorf, Publisher Phil Wagner, Springfield, IL (abelincoln.com); 38, Corbis; 40, Granger; 42, Granger; 45, Granger; 46 left, LOC; 46 right, LFF; 47 left, Granger; 47 right, Granger; 48, National Museum of American History, Smithsonian Institution; 50, Eon Images; 52, The New York Public Library/ Art Resource, NY; 57, LOC; 59, Corbis; 60, The Art Archive/ Culver Pictures; 62, Granger; 63, Collection of Keya Morgan, Lincolnimages.com, NYC; 67, LOC; 70, LFF; 70 center, Kent State University Museum, Gift of Ross Trump in memory of his mother Helen Watts Trump, 1994; 73 left, Public Domain; 73 center, Eon Images; 73 right, Eon Images; 75, Kent State University Museum, Gift of Ross Trump in memory of his mother Helen Watts Trump, 1994.

Published by the
National Geographic Society

John M. Fahey, Jr.,
President and Chief Executive Officer

Gilbert M. Grosvenor, *Chairman of the Board*

Tim T. Kelly, *President, Global Media Group*

John Q. Griffin, *President, Publishing*

Nina D. Hoffman, *Executive Vice
President; President, Book Publishing Group*

Staff for This Book

Nancy Laties Feresten, *Vice President,
Editor-in-Chief of Children's Books*

Bea Jackson, *Design and Illustrations
Director, Children's Books*

Jennifer Emmett, *Executive Editor*

Kate Waters, *Project Editor*

David M. Seager, *Art Director*

Lori Epstein, Charlotte Fullerton,
Illustrations Editors

Candace Hyatt, *Indexer*

Jennifer Thornton, *Managing Editor*

Grace Hill, *Associate Managing Editor*

R. Gary Colbert, *Production Director*

Lewis R. Bassford, *Production Manager*

Rachel Faulise, Nicole Elliott,
Manufacturing Managers

Susan Borke, *Legal and Business Affairs*

Founded in 1888, the National Geographic Society is
one of the largest nonprofit scientific and educational
organizations in the world. It reaches more than 285
million people worldwide each month through its official journal, National Geographic, and its four other
magazines; the National Geographic Channel; televi-
sion documentaries; radio programs; films; books; vid-
eos and DVDs; maps; and interactive media. National
Geographic has funded more than 8,000 scientific
research projects and supports an education program
combating geographic illiteracy.

For more information, please call
1-800-NGS LINE (647-5463)
or write to the following address:

National Geographic Society
1145 17th Street N.W.
Washington, D.C. 20036-4688 U.S.A.

Visit us online at www.nationalgeographic.com/books.
Librarians and teachers, visit us at
www.ngchildrensbooks.com.

Kids and parents, visit us at
kids.nationalgeographic.com.

For information about special discounts
for bulk purchases, please contact
National Geographic Books Special Sales:
ngspecsales@ngs.org.

For rights or permissions inquiries, please contact
National Geographic Books Subsidiary Rights:
ngbookrights@ngs.org.

Printed in U.S.A.